Make It HAPPEN!

"Big Boy" Wills

CARTOONIST

CLARENCE WILLS JR.

© C.W.

BY RYAN HUME

Lightswitch
LEARNING

150 East 52nd Street, Suite 32002
New York, NY 10022
www.lightswitchlearning.com

Educators and Librarians, for a variety of teaching resources, visit www.lightswitchlearning.com

Library of Congress Cataloging-in-Publication Data is available upon request.
Library of Congress Catalog Card Number pending

ISBN: 978-1-68265-582-5

2 3 4 5 6 7 8 9 10

"Big Boy" Wills by Ryan Hume

Edited by Lauren Dupuis-Perez
Book design by Sara Radka
The text of this book is set in Minion Pro Regular.

Printed in China

Image Credits

Cover: Big Boy Wills;
(background) Pixabay
Page 1: See credits for cover
Page 4: (all) Getty Images
Page 5: (all) Wills Family
Page 6: Wills Family
Page 7: Wills Family
Page 8: Wills Family
Page 9: Wills Family
Page 10: Wills Family
Page 11: Wills Family
Page 12: (top) Wills Family;
(bottom) Big Boy Wills
Page 13: Getty Images, iStockphoto
Page 14: Getty Images, Brand X
Page 15: Getty Images, Cultura RF
Page 16: Getty Images
Page 17: Wills Family
Page 18: (all) Big Boy Wills
Page 19: Getty Images, iStockphoto

Page 20: Big Boy Wills
Page 21: Getty Images, EyeEm
Page 22: Big Boy Wills
Page 23: Getty Images, Hero Images
Page 24: Getty Images, Westend61
Page 25: Getty Images
Page 26: Big Boy Wills
Page 27: Getty Images, iStockphoto
Page 28: (top) Getty Images, Scott
Morgan; (bottom) Big Boy Wills
Page 29: Getty Images, Cindy Ord
Page 30: Big Boy Wills
Page 31: Getty Images, Blend Images
Page 32: Wills Family
Page 33: Wills Family
Page 34: Wills Family
Page 35: Getty Images, iStockphoto:
Page 36–37: Big Boy Wills
Page 38: Getty Images, Mike Coppola
Page 39: Getty Images, Brand X

Page 40: Big Boy Wills
Page 41: Wills Family
Page 42: (all) Big Boy Wills
Page 43: (right) Getty Images,
iStockphoto; (left, top and
bottom) Big Boy Wills
Page 44: Wills Family
Page 45: Getty Images,
Stephen Shugerman
Page 45: Big Boy Wills
Page 46: Alonzo Boldin
Page 47: Getty Images
Page 48: (top) Getty Images; (bottom)
Getty Images, iStockphoto
Page 49: (top and middle) Big Boy Wills;
(bottom) Getty Images, Blend Images
Page 50: (left) Wills Family;
(right) iStockphoto
Page 51: (left) Big Boy Wills;
(right) Wills Family

"I'm just a happy guy at heart."

Clarence "Big Boy" Wills, Jr.

• • •

Make It HAPPEN!

Skills for Success

Both searching for and then working toward a career can be challenging work. This feature at the end of each chapter will help readers build toward career readiness. The "Make It Happen" activity will tie relevant information from every chapter into ideas about career readiness. It will enable readers to more easily reach a variety of personal and career goals to ensure success in school and in the community.

Contents

Introduction

Clarence "Big Boy" Wills, Jr., always has his pencils, pens, and a notebook with him. He has been drawing cartoons ever since he was a young boy. When he feels inspired—and he often is—he has the materials he needs. Big Boy draws for many hours every day.

When he was a child, Big Boy was **diagnosed** with **autism**. Autism affects the way a person sees and interacts with other people and the world around them. Big Boy interacts with the world by drawing cartoon characters. With the help of his pencils and his family, Big Boy has come out of his shell, turning his drawings into educational materials to help others that have had their lives affected by autism.

To become a cartoonist or artist means being disciplined, working hard, having a plan, and of course **collaborating** with others. Through this book, students will discover that every person has their very own unique measure of success.

Big Boy's cartoons are often just as happy and joyful as he is.

Big Boy has used his talent and love for drawing to help educate others about disabilities.

Big Boy grew up in a big family. By the time he was eight years old he had four siblings.

Who is Big Boy?

Big Boy was always treated like any other kid in the Wills family. He always enjoyed sitting on his dad's motorcycle with his sister.

Using blank paper and colored pens, Clarence Douglas "Big Boy" Wills quietly works at his desk. Day after day his dreams come alive as he skillfully turns them into reality. Slowly and with great care, his delicate hands draw the cartoons that he creates in his rich imagination. Big Boy Wills is a unique artist at work.

Big Boy was born in 1968. He was the second child of Clarence Douglas, Sr., and Ruth. His big sister, Cheryl, was born in 1966 and went on to become an award-winning journalist in New York City. Mrs. Wills was a stay-at-home mom, and Clarence was a New York City fireman. By the time Big Boy was six, the Wills family had grown even larger. Big Boy's sister, Crystal Dianne, was born in 1972. In 1974, twins Celestial Daphne and Cleavon Daryl were born. Big Boy's older sister, Cheryl, would later write in her book *Die Free*, "My mother loved my dad so much that she had given all of us names with his initials."

But Clarence, Jr., wouldn't be known by the initials C.D. for very long. Big Boy got his nickname from Cheryl when she was just a toddler. When he was born, he was a large baby. "He had big cheeks," Cheryl remembered. "Big hair. Lots of hair on his head. He was just thick and meaty. I just looked at him and thought he was a big boy."

The Wills family, including Big Boy's three sisters and younger brother, always supported him and surrounded him with love.

Big Boy's Family

When Big Boy was born, the Wills family lived in Rockaway Beach. It is a neighborhood in the New York City borough of Queens. The seaside community has a long boardwalk running along the beach. Far from the crowds of Manhattan, neighborhood kids happily run in the sand and chase the seagulls on the boardwalk. Looking east, the horizon seems to go on forever over the Atlantic Ocean.

But Big Boy was not like other kids. He stayed closer to home. He didn't have any friends. His mother began to worry about Big Boy early on. She became concerned when she saw big changes in his behavior. He stopped responding to his name. He stopped laughing and playing with his older sister. Big Boy's mother started to get help for her son when he was about three or four years old. "But I knew there was a problem earlier than that," she said. "He became withdrawn at an early age, about eighteen months."

CRASH COURSE IN CARTOONS

art exhibit: a limited-time presentation of artwork in a gallery space or museum

Bugs Bunny: an animated rabbit and star of the Looney Tunes cartoon universe

creative process: the stages artists go through when planning and creating art

display: to put something where people can see it

logo: a symbol that is used to identify a company and that appears on its products

Popeye the Sailor Man: a cartoon sailor with strong arms who encourages kids to eat spinach

sketch: to create a quick, rough drawing

technique: a way of doing something by using special knowledge or skill

Woody Woodpecker: an animated woodpecker known for his speed and tricky behavior

Clarence, Sr., Big Boy's father, was proud of his son.

Autism is what is known as a **Spectrum Disorder**. A spectrum is like a scale between one and ten. With autism, the lower side of the scale barely presents any symptoms or signs of autism. The higher side presents severe signs of autism.

Autism is a disorder that affects the way people develop **social skills**. People with autism may seem like they want to be alone or ignore others. They may also avoid eye contact. It is possible that they do not like to be touched. They could even get upset if their daily routine changes. Each case is different. Where one symptom is present in one person, it could be absent in another.

Discovering Autism

Mrs. Wills took Big Boy to many different doctors, hoping to better understand his situation. "They had the nerve to try and tell me he was deaf," Mrs. Wills said. "And I said, 'No, he doesn't have a hearing problem.'" Each new doctor couldn't figure out what was wrong with Big Boy. "They went from one solution to another, which proved not to be it." For several years he was never fully **diagnosed**. Still, he focused on cartoons and began his **creative process**.

Cheryl and Big Boy are close in age. They have a special bond that started when they were both just babies.

Big Boy was diagnosed with autism around the age of six. Today, doctors are learning more and more about autism, but they still don't know

CAPIN SQUIDD

what exactly causes it. It can still be hard to diagnose, as symptoms could be different for each patient. Back in the 1970s, when Big Boy was a child, doctors did not know a lot about autism in terms of treatment and managing the condition. People with autism often ended up being labeled with the wrong kind of disability, like deafness. **Misdiagnosis** could lead to more trouble down the road.

Even after his diagnosis, Big Boy's life didn't change very much at home. "I didn't allow my children to be treated differently," Mrs. Wills said. "And I certainly didn't treat them different. My kids are special children and they just embraced him, especially Cheryl. They taught him how to read, they taught him how to write, and, you know, retain his self-control."

Living With Autism

People with autism often express themselves differently to the outside world. People with autism frequently have trouble understanding social behavior like body language, facial expressions, and tone of voice. Further, people without autism may not understand similar attributes in those with autism, which can be confusing.

For instance, some people assume that people with autism do not want friends because they are quiet or distant. Most people with autism just have trouble making friends because they don't know how to reach out. Big Boy loves his family and takes his relationships seriously. One of the biggest mistakes people make about those with autism is that they are not smart. In fact, many people with autism excel in math, music, computers, or reading. Big Boy has always been curious and interested in the world. He has used drawing to explore and connect with the world around him.

Some kids are inspired by what they see and read in books.

Books and Art

The Wills family kept a library in their home and Big Boy grew up surrounded by books, records, and lots of family photos. He'd spend hours leafing through the books, touching each page. He would even sketch in blank pages of the books. This love of literature and different visuals led to an interest in art. Art became Big Boy's way to engage with the world.

The Wills kids made sure their brother was included in all parts of family life. "We didn't treat him like a special kid," Cheryl said. "In all honesty we didn't know what autism was anyway. He was fully included in everything we did—birthdays, holidays, everything." Mrs. Wills added, "If Big Boy wasn't invited, no one went."

Make It HAPPEN!

Respect Differences

At some point in your school or professional career you will have to discuss difficult topics or talk to people who may not agree with you. You can practice friendly debate with a friend.

Find a topic that you and your friend do not agree on. Then use these tips while discussing:

- Focus on what the other person has to say to help you understand them better.
- Listen carefully to the other person speaking. Respond with body language and facial expressions.
- When you are ready to respond, you should take as much time as you need to get your point across. Give **context** to your answers by explaining why you feel the way you do. Avoid harsh language that may make the other person feel defensive if you're having a difficult conversation.

How did it go? Ask your friend how they felt about the conversation. Were you able to have a disagreement and still listen?

First Steps of the Journey

Cartoons inspired Big Boy to create his own art.

Cartoon Craze

When Big Boy was growing up in the 1970s, television was not like it is today. There were no shows "on demand." You couldn't watch whatever you wanted whenever you wanted. TVs did not have two hundred-plus channels. Most televisions only had the three major networks—ABC, CBS, and NBC—until the 1980s, when cable grew popular.

Birthdays have always been a big deal in the Wills' house. Cheryl and Big Boy were buddies at every family event growing up.

Saturday morning cartoons began in the 1960s. In the 1970s, each of the three major television networks ran about four hours of cartoons between 8 a.m. and noon on Saturday mornings. This meant characters such as Scooby Doo or The Jetsons became a part of American culture. Some of the cartoon programs brought in more than twenty million viewers per week.

DID YOU KNOW?

The popular animated film, *Finding Dory*, is put together from 289,240,840 different pictures to make up one movie that is 1 hour and 38 minutes long.

As a kid, Big Boy watched cartoons like he was under a spell. "He loved cartoons," Mrs. Wills recalled. "He watched them differently than we watched them," Cheryl agreed. "We could watch them casually but he was intently focused and would not even turn his head from the TV when the cartoons were on."

An Artist Revealed

Although Big Boy did not talk much, he would try to copy the voices he heard coming from the television. This was around the time the doctors had said he might be deaf. Cheryl recalled, "He would raise his finger and pretend to write things in midair and drift off into his own world."

When Big Boy started drawing at four or five, he would scribble on blank pages of books in the family library. "He would just start making these circular motions," Cheryl described. "And he did it in every book my mother had. Like a spiral." Even now, as a grown-up artist, the signature he signs his drawings with ends with a scribble that looks like a little tornado. It is his signature touch.

Lardball, Super Stretch, and Pete Pretzel

Today, Big Boy wakes up in the morning, goes downstairs with a pad of paper, and draws something whenever he feels inspired. "He stops when he sleeps, he stops to watch a little television and read the newspaper," Cheryl said. "But other than that, he has a pencil in his hand, drawing." Even when he's in the car, he might draw. Big Boy usually associates everyone he sees with a cartoon, his mother said.

The Creative Process

The Creative process is how some artists develop their ideas in order to make a final product. Inspiration can lead to research and sometimes research can lead to inspiration. Creating something brand new, like a story or new piece of art, takes a lot of thought and brainstorming. For many, the creative process begins well before any art is actually created.

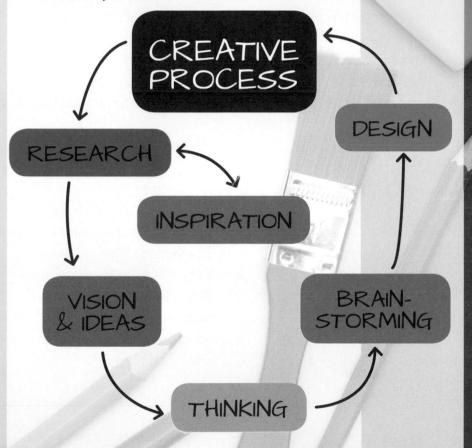

CREATIVE PROCESS

RESEARCH

DESIGN

INSPIRATION

VISION & IDEAS

BRAIN-STORMING

THINKING

Creating a Style

When Big Boy was young, there was a select group of characters he would draw regularly: **Woody Woodpecker**, **Bugs Bunny**, and **Popeye the Sailor Man**. "All of the cartoons he saw, he attempted to mimic them," Cheryl said. "None of us knew he was trying to express this creative spark. Eventually, we all got hip to the fact that this kid needs to have a book and a pencil or crayons with him all the time." Cheryl explained further that Big Boy literally taught himself to draw. "Doing it over and over again," she said, "he got really good at it."

"He started drawing his own cartoons to be buddies with them," Mrs. Wills said. "He made his own friends in cartoons. He made his own **security blanket**. Other than his sisters and his brother, the cartoons became his lifelong friends."

Big Boy got so passionate about learning how to draw his favorite cartoons that he didn't stop at just drawing the characters. Even when the show ended and names began to scroll across the screen he was carefully watching every word on the screen. "When the credits rolled, he memorized that too, and he knew every single voice of Bugs Bunny was being spoken by a man named Mel Blanc. [. . .] He can write out the credits to any cartoon."

CHET AND ZEKE

The Nutwits are some of Big Boy's original characters.

Big Boy got the support he needed at a school that focused on educating students with special needs. Overall, he did well. "He was surrounded by his peers," Mrs. Wills said. But even with all of his practice and talent, he didn't do so well in his art classes. "They wanted to tell him how to draw. And he already knew how to draw what he wanted to draw," she said. Sometimes artists take their own path and don't do well with traditional teaching. Many artists have already figured out their own methods at a young age. "It was like, in one ear [and] out the other," Cheryl added. "They wanted him to paint flowers. He didn't want to paint flowers. He wanted to create his characters."

DID YOU KNOW?

Bugs Bunny has his own star on the Hollywood Walk of Fame.

Art as Language

Abstract art is a type of painting that tries to use shapes, color, and texture to send a message in a new and unusual way. It is often up to the viewer to decide what it means. Some artists with autism have found success using abstract art to communicate their feelings with the world.

Niam Jain, a twelve-year-old boy with autism who lives in Toronto, Canada, has become an abstract painter. Though he doesn't talk very much, Jain has found that he can use painting to communicate with the world.

Iris Grace Halmshaw, who has autism, started doing art therapy when she was two years old. Her parents were so impressed with her work that they tried to sell some of her paintings. One painting she made when she was just three years old sold for 830 English pounds, which is more than one thousand dollars!

Finding His Voice

Big Boy began to respond to the world through the cartoons he saw and the drawings he made. He would recreate cartoon characters on the page and say they were friends of the ones on TV. He'd always begin drawing in pencil. Mrs. Wills said he'd create the characters in his own way, which truly impressed his mother. He did not quite excel in art class. Mrs. Wills explained that if Big Boy wasn't interested in the subject, he didn't want to draw it. But he did learn new **techniques**. Mrs. Wills believes he applied them to his own work. Eventually, he began creating his own characters, along with **logos** for contests. In the early 2000s, he started drawing people.

Big Red

Whenever Big Boy feels inspired, he'll jot his ideas down on a pad and a cartoon will come to life. His sister and mother say this is a staple of Big Boy's life.

Over the years, Big Boy has created hundreds of different cartoon characters. These include Peterkin and the Pixie Queen, Donny Dwarf, Elmer Elf, and Gandalf Gnome. "For most of my life I have been creating cartoon characters," Big Boy said. "One day I hope to be like the great Charles Schultz, who created the all-time favorite Peanuts characters. Snoopy was my favorite when I was a kid."

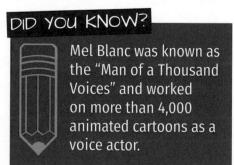

DID YOU KNOW?

Mel Blanc was known as the "Man of a Thousand Voices" and worked on more than 4,000 animated cartoons as a voice actor.

Make It! HAPPEN!

Create Art

Being able to think creatively and use your imagination takes practice. The more you think creatively, the easier it may become. **Creative thinking** can help with self-expression. Being able to use your **imagination** may also help you problem-solve in unique ways. It may also reveal a passion for the arts you didn't know was there. Complete one of the projects below to flex your creative muscle.

- Write a story based on the first picture you see in a nearby magazine.
- Draw your favorite place to visit or a moment from a recent trip.
- Write a poem about something or someone you love.

Did you work on something you have never tried before? Discuss with a friend or teacher how you felt about the creative process. Was it easier than you imagined? What parts challenged you?

3

Overcoming Obstacles

Big Boy creates all of his
drawings with pencil first.

Thriving Through Adversity

Big Boy's family always made sure that their brother had room to play where other kids didn't bother him. He was still able to play outside in the neighborhood and was surrounded by plenty of love and support at home.

DID YOU KNOW?

In the United States, people visit libraries three times more often than they go to the movies.

Safe spaces are important for people with autism because they can be overwhelmed by things that wouldn't bother someone else. Art and drawing can also act as a sort of safe space. By allowing Big Boy to draw and lead a full, healthy life, the Wills family was forming a safe space around him.

With a supportive home and the help of his peers at the Rosemary Kennedy School in Long island, New York, Big Boy started to come out of his shell. The school teaches students with moderate to severe learning disabilities. The school has students from kindergarten all the way through twelfth grade. Besides regular classes, students interact with their community. They go on field trips to places like the bowling alley or library. "They did a fantastic job on speech and everything else," Mrs. Wills said. "He started [speaking in] complete sentences and they taught him how to express himself."

Trips to the library were perfect for Big Boy, who always loved books.

Succeeding with Autism

Outside of the community trips, Big Boy also held a job at the local McDonalds for 10 years. He first started working there in his late teens, and continued into his mid- to late twenties. It provided structure and routine for Big Boy, who worked very hard. He took pride in his job and was respected by his coworkers and customers.

Big Boy is a thoughtful and considerate man, who is always thinking about his family. "Every birthday he draws a picture of whoever's birthday it is," Cheryl said. "He has four siblings, a mom, brothers-in-law, nieces, nephews, and every birthday [. . .] he never forgets." Big Boy draws personal birthday cards for everyone who is close to him. "He writes on the inside, 'A thousand congratulations,' and he knows exactly what age you are. If it's his nephew, he'll sign, 'Uncle Biggy,' something he calls himself."

Uncle Biggy

UNCLE BIGGY
THE MAGIC MOTION MAKER

Lasting Impact

Cartoons can be a large part of many people's childhoods. Many kids become attached to their favorite characters and look forward to their shows every week. Some cartoons have spanned multiple generations. This means that some adults can show their children the cartoons they used to watch when they were kids! These are the top five longest-running cartoons.

SHOW	SEASONS
Arthur	20
The Bugs Bunny and Tweety Show	14
Teenage Mutant Ninja Turtles	10
SpongeBob SquarePants	10
Rugrats	9

President Barack Obama was an inspiring figure for Big Boy. He became the spark that encouraged Big Boy to engage with the world through politics.

A Shift in Focus

One thing that surprised the entire family was when Big Boy got interested in politics. In 2007, when President Barack Obama began his first presidential campaign, Big Boy started to pay attention to the news. He was fascinated by the young candidate from Chicago. "He loved Woody Woodpecker, Charlie Brown, Bugs Bunny," Cheryl said, "but never a politician!"

The family had never seen him so interested in something outside of his private world. Big Boy went online to do research about Obama. He started reading the newspaper every day. "He wanted to know everything there was to know about President Barack Obama," Cheryl said.

President Barack Obama

Big Boy turned his focus to the campaign and began to produce a lot of campaign posters praising the election of President Barack Obama. His drawings of Obama were hung all over town, too. "Now he follows local races," Cheryl said. "He's stayed with it. He reads the papers. He watches the news. He watches CNN. He pays attention."

Success Stories

Many people on the autism spectrum go on to follow their passions and find success by overcoming their challenges. Daniel Wendler turned his challenges with learning social skills into a book called *Improve Your Social Skills*. He now speaks publicly on this subject across the country. Jacob Velazquez began playing the piano when he was three years old. He is now considered a **prodigy** at age seven and has performed on *Good Morning America* and elsewhere.

Jacob Velazquez

Diagnosed with autism at the age of two, Dr. Temple Grandin didn't speak until she was three and a half years old. She would go on to receive degrees in Psychology and Animal Science. She has been a professor at Colorado State University for the last two decades. She has consulted for a number of companies on animal welfare. Now half of the cattle in the whole country are managed by a program she designed. Grandin began speaking about autism in the 1980s and is one of the most well-known advocates on the subject

A Larger Worldview

Big Boy calls this drawing "Cheryl Wills, the All-American Working Girl."

Back in 2009, Cheryl actually got the chance to attend the historic **inauguration** of the 44th President of the United States, President Barack Obama, America's first African American president. "I was seated on the lawn of the United States capitol, in the VIP orange section, and thought of my little brother, Big Boy," Cheryl remembered in her book *Die Free*. "I called him every step of the way and said, 'Big Boy, I'm here—I'm freezing to death—but I'm here. I'm watching him being sworn in!' And my brother replied in his very unique speaking voice, 'Whoo hoo! Way to go, Sis!'"

DID YOU KNOW?

More than 1.8 million people attended President Barack Obama's first inauguration on January 20, 2009.

Make It! HAPPEN!

Become a Volunteer

Volunteering not only gives back to the community but is also a great way to show **initiative** and gain leadership skills. As the organization Autism Speaks says on its website, "Whether it's stuffing envelopes, identifying service providers, or chairing a walk, volunteers make the difference!"

To get started, here are some organizations that can always use a helping hand:

- Autism Speaks (www.autismspeaks.org). This large advocacy organization has local chapters all over the country seeking volunteers.

- Autism Society (www.autism-society.org). This organization started the Autism Source Resource Database in 2004. It is the largest collection of reliable resources and offers many volunteer opportunities.

- Create the Good (www.createthegood.org). This website has many opportunities and creative ways to get involved and help people with a range of disabilities.

Report back to a teacher, mentor, or parent. Where would you like to volunteer? What skills do you need to be a successful volunteer?

Teamwork

4

Cheryl and Big Boy continue to be an amazing team.

Making a Difference

Cheryl and Big Boy spoke at the International Sibling Conference.

In August 2010, Cheryl and Big Boy were the featured speakers at the International Sibling Conference in Greenwich, Connecticut. Cheryl spoke at the event. The conference is a meeting organized by the Sibling Leadership Network. Its goal is to promote the value of people with disabilities within their families and also to honor the siblings who accept and champion their brothers or sisters who have disabilities.

Cheryl spoke for a few minutes about their lives growing up together before she introduced her brother to the crowd. Big Boy walked to the podium through loud applause and, with confidence, softly said "Thank you" into the microphone.

DID YOU KNOW?

Seventy-four percent of people have what's called speech anxiety, or "glossophobia," meaning they're nervous when speaking in front of a crowd.

"Good evening," he continued. "My name is Clarence Wills and I am very happy to be here. I'm just a happy guy at heart. I have a pretty big family as you can see. My older sister Cheryl is like my best friend. Naturally, we are just like peas and carrots. She loves my artwork and tells me that I am going to be a great artist someday."

Co-Hosting

Cheryl and Big Boy worked together, introducing a concert at the Apollo Theater.

A few weeks before he gave his speech at the International Sibling Conference, Cheryl brought Big Boy to the stage at the legendary Apollo Theater in Harlem. Harlem is a neighborhood in New York City known for its roots in African American culture. Cheryl had been asked to serve as a host at a concert for two bands who have members with disabilities. Cheryl would later write in the *Huffington Post*, "Before I had agreed to **emcee** the event, I told event planners that I wanted my brother Clarence to co-host with me; I subtly indicated, 'No him—no me.'"

When they arrived, she saw that the Apollo was absolutely filled with people. She wondered if Big Boy would be nervous or startled. Cheryl recalled, "The little boy, who once banged his head against walls so violently that I had to physically restrain him from hurting himself, delivered his lines with ease, precision, and passion." It was another instance of **collaboration**. Big Boy was showing up as a teammate for his sister.

They have partnered with a number of organizations that deal with issues related to disabilities, including the AHRC. It is one of the largest **nonprofit** organizations in New York and works to promote "full" lives for those with disabilities. Big Boy produces educational materials and event posters for these organizations.

Cheryl has spent her entire life protecting Big Boy. She stood up to bullies, kept him from harming himself at times, and showed her siblings, by example, how to include Big Boy in everything they did. She has encouraged his art and is his biggest fan. "Being the oldest child you have a sense of protecting the little one," Cheryl said.

"What I do now is get him everything he wants," Cheryl said. "I buy all of his Christmas presents. After Halloween, he gives me a list of everything he has found online. I literally go right down the list and get him everything."

DID YOU KNOW?

Walt Disney's *Snow White and the Seven Dwarfs* was the first full-length cartoon ever released. It came out in 1937.

About Helping Others

- In the United States, 25 percent of people volunteer.
- On average, people around the world spend about five hours volunteering each month.
- People in the United States donate almost $140 billion every year.
- Around the world, 30 percent of people say they help a stranger every month.
- People in Australia help more strangers, donate more money, and volunteer more often than people in any other country.

Cast of Characters

The characters featured here are ones that Big Boy has created. He views them as friends, supporters, inspiration, and entertainers. They have made a large impact on his life.

PETERKIN

Peterkin is a character who does not behave well and bullies other kids. Peterkin was created so that kids can learn to be nice to others.

PIXIE QUEEN

Pixie Queen is a princess, a good person who taught Peterkin not to be a bully and to get along with all people.

DONNY DWARF

Donny Dwarf was created to teach kids to be nice and stay out of trouble. Big Boy believes that by keeping Donnie Dwarf in their minds, kids will be well-behaved.

ELMER ELF

Elmer Elf was created to help kids stay out of trouble and to keep good thoughts in their minds.

GANDALF GNOME

Gandalf Gnome was created to tell kids that there are no shortcuts in life. People must work hard to stay out of trouble and do well.

Big Sister Cheryl

Today, Big Boy is part of a **special needs center**. Cheryl explained, "They go on trips and I give him money to make sure he can go on the trip." She continued, "Any time he needs something extra, I get it for him. So in that way I am still protecting him."

Big Boy has become an irreplaceable teammate to his sister. Cheryl and Big Boy have shared their experiences through the stories they tell and through Big Boy's art. In doing so, he continues to prove that he is perfectly capable of taking on one new challenge after the next.

Cheryl Wills's Career

Big Boy's older sister, Cheryl Wills, is an award-winning television journalist based in New York City.

She is the author of several books, including *Die Free, The Emancipation of Grandpa Sandy Wills,* and most recently, *Emancipated: My Family's Fight for Freedom.* All of her books reveal her discovery that her great-great-great grandfather, Sandy Wills, was a slave who joined the U.S. Army to fight against the Confederacy during the Civil War (1861–1865).

Make It! HAPPEN!

Prepare a Speech

Public speaking is an important skill to have in building a career or collaborating with others. To become an effective speaker:

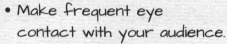

- Make frequent eye contact with your audience.
- Do not cross up your limbs (hands/legs) or twitch/rock too often.
- Use an "internal clock" to track your pace.
- Try to gauge the audience's reaction.
- Improvise only when necessary.

Now, prepare to make a speech. Suppose you are running for president or vice president of the student council. A part of the election process is making a speech in front of the student body. It has to be two minutes in length and must address your qualities as a leader and your plans.

DIZZY
BERNIE
CARRIE AARON
SKIPPER
HANK
BURRITO

BONEHEADS

DINGO
MELVIS
BAYWICK
BASIE JONES
ALI

PEPPER
ROXIE
T-BONE

DOBY

KIBBY
Boneheads Characters
PORSHIA   MUFFET   DANA
GATOR   KHAZZAM

"BONEHEADS"

Big Boy, Mrs. Wills, Cheryl

Big Boy Today

Every day Big Boy works hard and takes the initiative to be a successful cartoonist. Having the love and support of his family has made all the difference in Big Boy's life. Without his team of friends and family, Big Boy would not have been able to grow as an artist. With his mom and his sister always by his side, Big Boy continues to create his characters and cartoons. He has been able to find new places and events to display his art. He also continues to participate in public-speaking engagements.

Big Boy lives with his mother in Freeport, New York, on Long Island. "Where, oh where, would any of us be without our dear mothers?" Big Boy said to the crowd at the International Sibling Conference. "I don't know where I'd be without her."

DID YOU KNOW?

The popular 2016 movie *The Accountant,* starring Ben Affleck, finds Affleck's character dealing with autism and utilizing his impressive skill for mathematics.

Giving Back With Art

Big Red

Flub-A-Dub and Eric Ermont

King Larz

Big Boy still spends hours drawing every day. His artwork is frequently displayed in AHRC New York centers across the greater New York City area. His cartoons are also hanging in many local libraries around Long Island. He was even part of an **art exhibit** at Hofstra University in Long Island, New York. An art exhibit is a limited-time special showing of artwork or other special objects in either a gallery space or a museum. Big Boy also sells his art at art fairs around New York.

Big Boy also won a contest to redesign a logo for the New York State Office of Vocational and Educational Services for Individuals with Disabilities (VESID). VESID works to find work for disabled New Yorkers. Every year, the department helps thousands of New Yorkers across the state find new jobs and become independent. When they chose Big Boy's design, the state of New York flew him up to Albany, the capital city of New York, to receive a plaque for his work.

The Fox Tops

Fluey

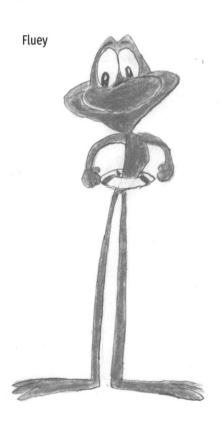

Best in the Biz

WALT DISNEY
Net Worth: $5 billion
Known for: Mickey Mouse, Donald Duck, Goofy, Pluto

MATT GROENING
Net Worth: $500 million
Known for: *The Simpsons*

WILLIAM HANNA AND JOSEPH BARBERA
Net Worth: $300 million
Known for: *The Flintstones, Tom & Jerry, The Jetsons, Scooby Doo, Huckleberry Hound*

JOHN LASSETER
Net Worth: $100 Million
Known for: *Cars, Toy Story, A Bug's Life*

At the International Sibling Conference, Big Boy met actor Chris Burke. Chris has down syndrome, but that has not stopped him from achieving his dreams.

Teamwork Continues

In addition to the Apollo Theater concert that he co-hosted with Cheryl and the International Sibling Conference where he spoke, Cheryl and Big Boy continue to collaborate on a variety of different projects. Together, they co-hosted the ReelAbilities: NY Disabilities Film Festival. This event celebrates films that tell the stories of people with disabilities.

They also hosted a gala for AABR that Big Boy created flyers for. The AABR is an organization that works with children and adults with disabilities to get them quality educations, housing, jobs, and more. Cheryl and Big Boy also created a school workbook for first, second, and third graders that teaches students the truth about people with disabilities.

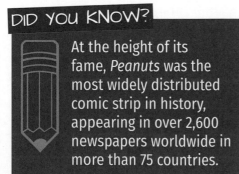

DID YOU KNOW?

At the height of its fame, *Peanuts* was the most widely distributed comic strip in history, appearing in over 2,600 newspapers worldwide in more than 75 countries.

Gene Gaylord and
Tony Flip

Chance Raspberry

No one expected Chance Raspberry to amount to anything. As a child with Tourette's Syndrome, he concentrated on drawing. When he felt alone, he focused on cartoons and continued to practice. Sixteen years later, Raspberry found himself drawing the ultimate bad boy, Bart Simpson, on the Emmy Award–winning animated show *The Simpsons*. "I think as a kid who had these feelings of being an outsider and being different, I loved watching Bart getting into trouble and seeing these stories told through the eyes of someone my age," Raspberry told *Upworthy* magazine.

When Big Boy and Cheryl spoke at the Apollo, the entire Wills family was there for support.

All in the Family

The Wills family has gotten bigger, too. Big Boy doesn't just have his mom, three sisters, and a brother anymore, but now he also has brothers-in-law and nieces and nephews. "I am really happy to have four siblings," Big Boy said at the International Sibling Conference. "They have always been there for me and I will always be there for them."

DID YOU KNOW?

A recent government survey of parents indicated that 1 in 45 children ages 3 to 17 have been diagnosed with autism spectrum disorder.

With a group as tight-knit as the Wills family, there is no doubt that Clarence "Big Boy" Wills, Jr., will have the support to keep working on his art and creating new characters that please and entertain viewers of all kinds.

Make It HAPPEN!

Collaborate As a Team

Imagine you are a skilled and respected researcher set to make a presentation at an annual conference about autism. Your research specialty is autism—its symptoms, attributes, treatment, history, etc. However, you are just one of three researchers in the presentation. Put together a clear, five-minute discussion about the condition. Each team member's specialty is a bit different. You'll have to collaborate on the project.

- Make an agreed-upon outline for the presentation.
- Discuss any mixed feelings or "question marks" about the subject matter.
- Question established conclusions, ideas, concepts, etc.
- Examine your teammates' evidence. Is it reputable? Reviewed?
- Peer review each other's writings/notes for the presentation in a timely manner.
- Run through your schedule before you take the stage.

How did it go? Did you find that you can be a helpful teammate?

Career Spotlights

Art has always been at the center of Big Boy's life. It has also opened the door for unique connections with his family and different opportunities in his life. These are some of Big Boy's major milestones throughout his experience as a cartoonist.

Artist

At age four, Big Boy discovers drawing, as doctors believe him to be deaf.

Young Cartoonist

When Big Boy is six years old, he draws his first cartoons, inspired by TV cartoons.

Birthday Card Designer
Big Boy makes his first birthday cards for family members when he is 17 years old.

Gallery Artist
When he is 23 years old, Big Boy's cartoons are displayed in art galleries in Long Island, New York.

Lesson Designer
Big Boy, 49, and Cheryl create materials to be sold in schools to help kids better understand learning challenges.

Defining Moments

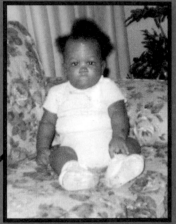

Big Boy begins to display signs of autism; he also takes a liking to drawing.

1972

Big Boy encounters bullies and continues to be protected by his sister Cheryl.

1974

Big Boy begins to take an interest in drawing cartoons.

1975

1980

Big Boy learns to speak and interact with others while at the Rosemary Kennedy School.

2007

Big Boy becomes interested in politics and draws posters of President Barack Obama.

2010

Big Boy first speaks to audiences about his family, learning challenges, and cartoons.

Depth of Knowledge Questions

1 How do you perceive the impact Saturday morning cartoons had on Big Boy's life? Draw examples from the text to support your answer.

2 Analyze in detail the author's representation of how a person with autism interacts with the world. How is the concept introduced and how is it later elaborated? What conclusions can you make?

3 What different skills enable Big Boy to be a successful cartoonist?

4 What is your opinion on the best way to learn a new skill, such as drawing? Make a claim and then write an argument to support it, using details and examples from the text.

5 Write a narrative describing an average day for Big Boy. Be sure to include specific details on how he creates a new cartoon, works on collaborative projects with his sister Cheryl, and furthers awareness of autism and other disabilities.

Prepare an Art Portfolio

Gather a team of classmates to create a group art portfolio. Artists use portfolios to showcase their work when applying for jobs or selling their art.

WHAT YOU NEED

- Artwork from school and home
- Art tools, such as colored pencils or markers
- Folder or binder

WHAT TO DO

1   Gather the artwork you have created for the Make It Happen! features within this book, plus other artwork from school and home.

2   Have each member explain the value and contribution of their pieces.

3   Collaborate to arrange a cohesive portfolio, using a folder or binder. Design and create an artistic cover for the portfolio.

4   What type of creative jobs could you apply for with this team? Come up with a marketing strategy for your group's portfolio and the skills it represents.

5   Collaborate to prepare a 10-minute presentation for a prospective employer. Highlight the skills required for a successful career and how they are reflected by the portfolio.

Glossary

art exhibit *(noun)* a limited-time presentation of artwork in a gallery space or museum (pg. 11)

autism *(noun)* a condition or disorder that begins in childhood and that causes problems in forming relationships and in communicating with other people (pg. 6)

collaborate *(verb)* to work with another person or group in order to achieve or do something (pg. 6)

context *(noun)* the group of conditions that exist where and when something happens (pg. 15)

creative process *(noun)* the stages artists go through when planning and creating art (pg. 11)

diagnose *(verb)* to recognize a disease or problem by examining someone (pg. 6)

display *(verb)* to put something where people can see it (pg. 11)

emcee *(noun)* a person who introduces speakers, players, or entertainers (pg. 34)

engage *(verb)* to give serious attention to (pg. 14)

inauguration *(noun)* the introduction of someone (such as a newly elected official) into a job or position with a formal ceremony (pg. 30)

initiative *(noun)* the determination to learn new things and improve skill levels on your own; the ability to get things done (pg. 31)

journalist *(noun)* the activity or job of collecting, writing, and editing news stories for newspapers, magazines, television, the internet, or radio (pg. 9)

logo *(noun)* a symbol that is used to identify a company and that appears on its products (pg. 11)

misdiagnosis *(noun)* an incorrect conclusion about the cause of a disease or problem (pg. 12)

nonprofit *(adjective)* not existing or done for the purpose of making money (pg. 34)

prodigy *(noun)* a young person who is unusually talented in some way (pg. 29)

safe space *(noun)* a place or environment in which a person can feel that they will not be exposed to discrimination, criticism, harassment, or any other emotional or physical harm (pg. 25)

security blanket *(noun)* a blanket that is carried by a child because it makes the child feel safe (pg. 20)

sketch *(verb)* to create a quick, rough drawing (pg. 11)

social skills *(noun)* the skills used to communicate and interact with other people, both verbally and through gestures and body language (pg. 11)

special needs center *(noun)* a place where those with disabilities can receive training, social interaction, and resources (pg. 38)

spectrum disorder *(noun)* a complete range of different experiences, emotions, or opinions (pg. 11)

technique *(noun)* a way of doing something by using special knowledge or skill (pg. 11)

Read More

Brooks, Josiah. *Draw With Jazza—Creating Characters: Fun and Easy Guide to Drawing Cartoons and Comics Paperback.* New York: Impact Books: 2016.

Hart, Christopher. *Modern Cartooning: Essential Techniques for Drawing Today's Popular Cartoons.* New York: Watson-Guptill Publications, 2013.

Higashida, Naokia. *Reason I Jump: the Inner Voice of a Thirteen-Year-Old Boy with Autism.* New York: Random House, 2013.

McHenry, Irene. *The Autism Playbook for Teens: Imagination-Based Mindfulness Activities to Calm Yourself, Build Independence, and Connect with Others.* Oakland, Calif.: Instant Help Books, 2014.

Poole, Hilary W., *Disability and Families.* Broomall, Pa.: Mason Crest, 2017.

Internet Links

https://www.animaker.com/

http://www.wedrawanimals.com/how-to-draw-woody-woodpecker/

http://www.bigblogcomics.com/2014/10/bugs-and-co-via-don-gunn.html

http://www.parents.com/parenting/better-parenting/style/volunteer-with-your-kids/

https://www.autismspeaks.org/blog/2015/04/28/qa-creator-teens-guide-autism

http://kidshealth.org/en/teens/autism.html?ref=search

Bibliography

Bose, Talika. "A 'Simpsons' animator's real-life struggle inspired a cartoon for kids with disabilities." *Upworthy.* Cloud Tiger Media, Inc., 02 Dec. 2016. Web. 30 June 2017.

Cheryl Wills. "International Sibling Conference." *YouTube.* YouTube, 01 Sept. 2010. Web. 30 June 2017.

Kashinsky, Lisa. "Making safe spaces for children with autism." *Eagle-Tribune.* Eagle-Tribune, 10 Apr. 2016. Web. 30 June 2017.

"Signs of Autism." *National Autism Association RSS.* National Autism Association, 2017. Web. 30 June 2017.

Wills, Cheryl. "Siblings on the Frontlines for People With Disabilities." *The Huffington Post.* Oath, Inc., 25 Aug. 2010. Web. 30 June 2017.

Wills, Cheryl. *Die Free: a Heroic Family History.* Minneapolis: Hillcrest Media Group, 2011. Print.

Index